Times Mirror Training Group

Times Mirror
Training Group

John H. Zenger
President, Training Group
The Times Mirror Company

Dear Reader,

Skills training leads to job success because training enables you to do your job easier, faster, and better. My unhesitating advice to anyone in the work force today is to constantly learn new skills. Don't stop with merely learning about *your* job. The people who contribute the most are those who understand the jobs of people around them, plus their own.

With skills training, you reap personal benefits. You'll feel more confident and your work will be infinitely more enjoyable and satisfying.

Your organization wins too. It becomes more competitive because the quality of products and services surges ahead when an organization has skilled employees. That's why training is a key priority.

The Business Skills Express series is designed to be an important aspect of your long-term career development. Whether you use these books in a formal training program or study them on your own, this fast-paced series gives you the tools to advance your career.

Organizations must change in order to prosper—and organizations change because people change. That's what the Business Skills Express Series is all about.

John H. Zenger

Zenger-Miller, Inc.
Kaset International
Learning International, Inc.

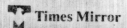
Times Mirror

THE NEW SUPERVISOR
Skills for Success

THE NEW SUPERVISOR
Skills for Success

BRUCE B. TEPPER

The Business Skills Express Series

BUSINESS ONE IRWIN/MIRROR PRESS
Burr Ridge, Illinois
New York, New York
Boston, Massachusetts

This symbol indicates that the paper in this book is made of recycled paper. Its fiber content exceeds the recommended minimum of 50% waste paper fibers as specified by the EPA.

This publication is designed to provide accurate and authoritative information in regard to the subject matter covered. It is sold with the understanding that neither the author nor the publisher is engaged in rendering legal, accounting, or other professional service. If legal advice or other expert assistance is required, the services of a competent professional person should be sought.

From a Declaration of Principles jointly adopted by a Committee of the American Bar Association and a Committee of Publishers.

Mirror Press:	David R. Helmstadter
	Carla F. Tishler
Editor-in-chief:	Jeffrey A. Krames
Project editor:	Jess Ann Ramirez
Production manager:	Diane Palmer
Interior designer:	Jeanne M. Rivera
Cover designer:	Tim Kaage
Art coordinator:	Heather Burbridge
Illustrator:	Boston Graphics, Inc.
Compositor:	TCSystems, Inc.
Typeface:	12/14 Criterion
Printer:	Malloy Lithographing, Inc.

Library of Congress Cataloging-in-Publication Data

Tepper, Bruce B.
    The new supervisor : skills for success / Bruce B. Tepper.
       p.   cm.—(Business skills express series)
    ISBN 1-55623-762-6
    1. Supervision of employees. 2. Self-evaluation. I. Title.
  II. Series.
    HF5549.12.T46   1994
               658.3'02—dc20   93–22351

Printed in the United States of America
2 3 4 5 6 7 8 9 0 ML 0 9 8 7 6 5 4 3

PREFACE

Congratulations on your new position as a supervisor! If this is your first opportunity to supervise the activity of others, you're undoubtedly looking forward to the experience.

For many, supervising others brings a mix of anticipation and fear. There is the promotion to the new position itself, the opportunity to teach others and share your knowledge—a new sense of authority and control.

There is also the fear of having to depend on others to do the work, of getting their respect and attention—of being responsible for what others do.

You'll find that there is no magic to being a good or even great supervisor. It takes some understanding of human behavior combined with the timely application of effective management skills.

If today is your first day on the job, this book can help you make some sense of your new responsibilities. It can help you develop your own program for success.

If you are a seasoned veteran, this book should provide you with some new approaches and ideas. It can help reinforce your efforts to become an even better supervisor.

You're on your way to learning and using the tools to ensure your success as an effective supervisor who is sought after by management and respected by employees. Good Luck!

Bruce B. Tepper

ABOUT THE AUTHOR

Bruce B. Tepper is a noted speaker, trainer, and consultant in management, marketing, and general business, specializing in the travel and incentive industries. Based in San Francisco, Mr. Tepper is an associate of R. W. & Associates of Scottsdale, Arizona, and has over 20 years of consulting, training, management, and marketing experience. Mr. Tepper's clients have included major hotel chains, computer reservations systems, travel agency groups, tourist boards, and other businesses using travel or incentive services.

Mr. Tepper is the author of *Incentive Travel: The Complete Guide,* as well as numerous articles and columns in industry magazines. As a member of the National Speakers Association and the Academy of Professional Consultants and Advisors, Mr. Tepper is a certified professional consultant (CPC). He holds an M.B.A. and an M.A. in teaching and education and is currently on the faculties of Golden Gate University, San Francisco State University, and the American Society of Travel Agents.

ABOUT
BUSINESS ONE IRWIN

Business One Irwin is the nation's premier publisher of business books. As a Times Mirror company, we work closely with Times Mirror training organizations, including Zenger-Miller, Inc., Learning International, Inc., and Kaset International to serve the training needs of business and industry.

About the Business Skills Express Series

This expanding series of authoritative, concise, and fast-paced books delivers high-quality training on key business topics at a remarkably affordable cost. The series will help managers, supervisors and frontline personnel in organizations of all sizes and types hone their business skills while enhancing job performance and career satisfaction.

Business Skills Express books are ideal for employee seminars, independent self-study, on-the-job training, and classroom-based instruction. Express books are also convenient-to-use references at work.

CONTENTS

Self-Assessment

How do you rate your supervising ability? This self-assessment will confirm your confidence or suggest areas for improvement. In either case, it is a starting point for progressing toward becoming a highly effective supervisor. For each statement, check off the category that best describes you.

	Always	Sometimes	Never
1. I feel comfortable in a leadership position.	_____	_____	_____
2. I am well organized in my activities.	_____	_____	_____
3. I plan my work activities in advance.	_____	_____	_____
4. I am comfortable making decisions.	_____	_____	_____
5. I can handle more than one project at a time.	_____	_____	_____
6. I organize my time well.	_____	_____	_____
7. I have good written communication skills.	_____	_____	_____
8. I have good oral communication and presentation skills.	_____	_____	_____
9. I am comfortable selling my ideas to others.	_____	_____	_____
10. People see me as a leader in group activities.	_____	_____	_____
11. I am a good teacher; people learn from me easily.	_____	_____	_____
12. I have a good understanding of people and am patient when working with others.	_____	_____	_____
13. I am comfortable sharing the workload with others.	_____	_____	_____
14. I am willing to take responsibility for the actions of others.	_____	_____	_____
15. I am willing to put in extra hours on the job when necessary.	_____	_____	_____
16. I enjoy solving problems involving human behavior.	_____	_____	_____
17. I can focus on long-range problems as well as day-to-day problems to help find solutions.	_____	_____	_____

To determine your score, give yourself a 3 for each Always, a 2 for each Sometimes, and a 1 for each Never. Now let's see how you did:

42 or higher   **Excellent skills.**

33–42   **Better than average but with room for improvement.**

24–32   **Average performance for a supervisor with several years' experience.**

32 or less   **Not unusual for the new supervisor.**

The Art of Supervising

Will you find all the answers you need in this book? Probably not. Supervision is as much an art as a science. With practice and experience, you'll gain confidence and better skills for handling the wide variety of challenges you're likely to encounter.

THE NEW SUPERVISOR
Skills for Success

1

The Role of the New Supervisor

This chapter will help you to:

- Understand the overall role of the supervisor.
- Develop personal plans and business plans.
- Decide how to put your plans into action.

Maria has worked in the clothing store for almost two years and has just been promoted to a supervisory position. She believes her promotion was the result of her excellent sales record (she often led the entire store) and her attention to customer service. Although she's never had management or supervisory training of any kind, she is excited—and nervous—about her new assignment. The promotion was a great opportunity. Now Maria's beginning to think about her new job and her career prospects. ■

THE NEW SUPERVISOR: GETTING STARTED

The role of the supervisor is, of course, "supervision." As a supervisor, you do your job by creating output through the efforts of others.

Your specific duties as a supervisor can include any or all of the following:

- Planning activities, hours, scheduling.
- Providing leadership and direction.
- Managing or supervising others to make sure work gets done.
- Taking responsibility for the performance of the people working for you.

How do you begin? Getting started as a supervisor should begin with

1

planning—both personal planning and business planning. If your business objectives don't mesh with your personal plans, it's time to rethink your goals.

CRITICAL QUESTIONS FOR PLANNING

Take time now to formulate your personal and business goals.

What Are My Long-Range Personal Goals?

Check the goals that apply to you. Add other goals you may have:

- ☐ Own my home
- ☐ Have a family
- ☐ Buy a new car
- ☐ Advance within the company
- ☐ Earn more money
- ☐ Have more prestige
- ☐ Other(s): _____

What Are the Business Goals for My Department and for Me, as a New Supervisor?

Check off your department's goals as well as your own.

- ☐ Earn the respect of my employees
- ☐ Eliminate problem situations
- ☐ Assert my authority
- ☐ Contribute great new ideas
- ☐ Change procedures and methods
- ☐ Convince top management of department's value and contribution
- ☐ Other(s): _____

What Are My Personal and Business Goals for Next Year and the Next Five Years?

List the goals in order of priority. Do your business goals mesh with your personal goals? Are they compatible with each other?

Next Year	Next Five Years
Personal Goals	
1.	1.
2.	2.
3.	3.
4.	4.
5.	5.

Next Year	Next Five Years
Business Goals	
1.	1.
2.	2.
3.	3.
4.	4.
5.	5.

What Action Must I Take to Get My Ideas and Plans Accepted?

☐ Get employee support
☐ Convince senior management
☐ Convince my boss
☐ Convince myself
☐ Other(s): _____

Of these actions, which one seems most crucial to you?

Implementing change is a way for new supervisors to not only enhance their careers but, more important, to improve the way their companies do business. Change can involve any of the actions you noted above.

PERSONALITY TRAITS OF THE SUCCESSFUL SUPERVISOR

Managers and supervisors need a variety of personality traits or characteristics to be successful. Check the traits that you see in yourself:

☐ Patience
☐ Tolerance
☐ Sensitivity
☐ Empathy
☐ Punctuality
☐ Decisiveness

What other traits do you think effective supervisors need?

_____

What areas do you need to improve?

_____

IMPEDIMENTS TO SUCCESS

What pitfalls can prevent your success as a supervisor? Check the impediments that may apply to you:

☐ Too many goals
☐ Lack of priorities
☐ Incomplete projects
☐ Lack of confidence
☐ Other(s): _____

We often feel frustrated in our attempts to reach new goals, and impediments such as those listed above are often the cause. In Chapter 2 and Chapter 5, we'll cover ways to overcome these typical impediments to success.

- Not prioritizing your goals' importance or leaving projects unfinished can both contribute to failure. You *must* evaluate each goal in relation to other goals and rank them in order of urgency.

- You must feel confident in your ability. Being self-motivated and self-disciplined is essential for your success.

YOUR ACTION PLAN AS A SUPERVISOR

Complete the following personal and business action plan. This is the first step toward becoming an effective supervisor. Your action plans will guide you through the everyday challenges of your new job.

1

Supervisor's Action Plan

1. List in order of priority the goals you've set for your department over the next year:

   _____   _____   _____
   _____   _____   _____
   _____   _____   _____
   _____   _____   _____
   _____   _____   _____

2. List the steps needed to accomplish each goal. (Repeat these steps for each goal.)

   Goal 1 is: _____
   _____
   _____

   Step 1. _____
   _____
   _____
   _____
   _____
   _____

   Step 2. _____
   _____
   _____
   _____
   _____
   _____

3. Evaluate your ability to attain each goal. Your job description and duties are a good place to start. (Write your own job description and list of duties if your company doesn't have one.)

   _____
   _____
   _____
   _____
   _____
   _____
   _____
   _____
   _____
   _____

1

4. Explore your resources. For each goal, what will you need to realize it?

_____

_____

_____

_____

_____

_____

_____

_____

5. Break down each goal into parts and establish a time frame for accomplishing them.

Goal 1 is: _____

_____

_____

Start date (to begin work): _____

Completion date: _____

Step 1. _____

_____

_____

_____

_____

_____

Step 2. _____

_____

_____

_____

_____

_____

6. Develop a way to measure and monitor progress toward each of your goals.

_____

_____

_____

_____

_____

_____

_____

_____

_____

PUTTING THE ACTION PLAN TO WORK

Now, what about putting the action plan to work? Let's return to Maria, our new department supervisor in the clothing store, to see what she does.

In setting her goals, Maria is careful to make them specific and realistic:

Unreasonable Goals	Reasonable Goals
Increase sales	Increase sales by a specific amount
Get everyone to like me	Earn the respect of my employees
Improve employee skills	Teach employees specific new skills

Maria established the goal of increasing her department's sales by 10 percent over the next year. That is her number one objective, and she strongly feels she can do it. This number one goal fits well into Maria's overall personal and departmental goals.

What steps might Maria take to make her goal a reality? The steps could include increasing the size of her staff, getting the company to do more advertising, improving the sales skills of her staff through training, adding new products, doing in-store promotions for her department, and so on.

It's impossible to answer question 3 (ability to succeed) on the Action Plan without considering question 4 (resources) as well. Can Maria succeed in her goal? It will greatly depend on her resources. Does the company have the financing to add more people and increase advertising? What other resources might she need?

Maria decides to improve the selling skills of her employees. The steps she decides to take are:

1. Determine the specific skills her staff needs (customer service, courtesy, closing sales, etc.).

2. Determine where and how those skills can be learned (seminars, video- or audiotapes, books, etc.).

3. Determine which method or program will best meet her staff's needs.

4. Evaluate her resources to make it happen.
   a. Is this goal in the scope of her job and duties?
   b. Will the company allocate the necessary funds?

    c. Will the employees have the time?

    d. Will the employees share her motivation and have a reason to improve? (If not, Maria will need to examine this problem as a separate issue.)

5. Break the training task down into its components.
   a. Select the best method for her company.
   b. Convince employees and management that this method is the best choice, with supporting reasons.
   c. Determine who will go through the program and then schedule training.

6. Set up a method to evaluate the effects of her training program:
   a. Determine everyone's current sales record.
   b. Measure everyone's sales on a month-to-month or week-to-week basis against their current performance.
   c. Observe whether employees are applying the new skills. If they are not, determine the reasons why and seek ways to motivate these employees.

Now that Maria has her plans all mapped out, she can get started and make modifications as needed.

How to Get Started

Let's review the basics of getting started in a supervisory job:

1. Determine personal and business goals for a one-year period and a five-year period.

2. Determine resources for reaching those goals (what new skills, abilities, and ideas, will you need?).

3. Break down and prioritize your objectives.

4. Get support for your goals from your employees and superiors.

5. Make decisions and implement plans to reach your goals.

Chapter Checkpoints

✓ Did you list your personal short- and long-term goals?

✓ Do your personal goals mesh with your business goals?

✓ What are your most important goals on the job (in order of importance)?

✓ What are the component parts of each goal?

✓ Is each goal realistic and attainable as defined?

✓ What resources will be needed to accomplish each goal?

2 | Leadership

This chapter will help you to:

- Evaluate the needs of your employees.
- Take inventory of your leadership skills.
- Consider ways to establish and exercise authority.

Tomio started as a clerical worker at the insurance company about three years ago. Everyone liked Tomio and felt he was good at his job. His supervisor was promoted, and Tomio was offered the position of supervising six other clerical workers, including some who've become good friends since he started the job.

Although Tomio has taken a couple of management courses in school, he's very concerned about his ability to lead others. He's a bit worried about how to work with people who are his friends as well as co-workers. Tomio wanted this position very much. In fact, his goals include advancing to management. Now that he's arrived, how can he win the respect of his staff and feel comfortable leading them? ■

PROMOTIONS WITHIN A COMPANY

If you've been promoted from within, it's time to take stock of your new role. Your former "equals" may, in some cases, resent your promotion. Others may feel that as their friend, you will give them favorable assignments or excuse unacceptable work habits.

For that reason, you must establish your position quickly. Your first duty is to do your job and do it well. That often means co-workers will no longer be close friends. You cannot put friendship above responsibility. That does not mean everyone will turn their back on you. Many will be proud and happy for you and will do everything they can to support you

2

in your new role. But do not stake your future on trying to stay friends with everyone and being a success as a supervisor at the same time. It is not possible.

The key to making a successful transition in the same workplace is to be clear about your own duties and responsibilities and about how best to go about your job.

THE SKILLS OF LEADERSHIP

Establishing your new role begins with a very vague term: *leadership*. Essentially, leadership is getting others to want to follow your direction and be productive in doing so.

Here are the skills necessary for leadership in most fields. Check those you feel you currently have:

Y	N	Confidence in your own ability
Y	N	Good communication skills
Y	N	The ability to make decisions
Y	N	Trust in your employees to do the job
Y	N	A desire to develop skills in others
Y	N	Comfortable in giving direction to others
Y	N	Ability to motivate people
Y	N	Other(s): _____

Why are these skills and traits important? Let's take a closer look at each one.

Confidence Is Important Because

- Others won't feel confident in a leader who lacks confidence.
- It subtly demonstrates your right to authority.
- It makes your subordinates feel comfortable that there is direction and purpose for what they do.

Good Communication Skills Are Essential to

- Clearly explain tasks and objectives to your subordinates.
- Provide guidance and direction on completing those tasks.
- Explain your actions to your superiors effectively.

Senior executives at major companies often cite their ability to make decisions as the main reason for their success.

Making Decisions Is Critical for

- Keeping the workflow moving.
- Quickly settling what could become major "personality" issues.
- Keeping the effort of all employees flowing in the same direction.

Trusting Your Employees Is Essential for

- The company to grow and expand.
- You and your employees to become more productive.
- Developing more skilled talent from within.

A Desire to Develop Skills in Others

- Helps them develop their own talents.
- Helps you tolerate mistakes that allow for growth and learning.
- Makes you a teacher as well as a supervisor—a person willing to share growth and recognition with others.

Feeling Comfortable in Giving Direction to Others

- Requires enormous patience with different individuals' abilities to learn new ideas and methods.
- Requires the communication skills already mentioned.
- Requires a coordinated effort with other supervisors and managers.

MOTIVATION

One leadership skill, motivation, deserves a closer look, since all other skills depend on this one. People are motivated by different needs: security, recognition, a sense of accomplishment, money, and the social aspects of their job, among others. Effective supervisors learn to recognize these characteristics and use the appropriate motivation with each employee.

As a supervisor, do not assume everyone shares your goals and desires. Not everyone wants the "headaches" of supervision or management. Many prefer to do the best possible work in their current job. It's your job to learn what each of your employees wants out of their work and what is important to them.

Many supervisors and managers assume their employees are driven by a desire for more money. Extensive research over the years has shown that money is usually *not* one of the top three motivators. More important to most people are recognition for doing a good job, opportunities for advancement, trust and responsibility, and respect. We'll look at motivation more closely in Chapter 11.

STEPS FOR DETERMINING EMPLOYEE NEEDS

Using the following worksheet, go through these three simple steps to determine the needs of the people who work for you:

1. List each employee and, from your perspective, write down what you feel are their top job goals.

2. Ask each employee what his or her goals are and compare the answers to your list. If you see a discrepancy, adjust your list and determine which goals are the best match. (Some employees may not have clearly defined goals or may prefer to tell you what they think you want to hear.)

3. List the steps you feel you can take to best meet each employee's needs in terms of your supervisory style.

Worksheet

Employee Name:	Goals		Best Course of Action
	Employee View	My View	
_____	_____	_____	_____
_____	_____	_____	_____
_____	_____	_____	_____
_____	_____	_____	_____
_____	_____	_____	_____
_____	_____	_____	_____
_____	_____	_____	_____
_____	_____	_____	_____
_____	_____	_____	_____
_____	_____	_____	_____
_____	_____	_____	_____
_____	_____	_____	_____
_____	_____	_____	_____
_____	_____	_____	_____
_____	_____	_____	_____
_____	_____	_____	_____
_____	_____	_____	_____
_____	_____	_____	_____
_____	_____	_____	_____
_____	_____	_____	_____
_____	_____	_____	_____
_____	_____	_____	_____
_____	_____	_____	_____
_____	_____	_____	_____
_____	_____	_____	_____
_____	_____	_____	_____

MEETING EMPLOYEE NEEDS

Psychological researchers have developed a variety of personality profiles and ways to evaluate people. As a supervisor, you need to be concerned with employee behaviors and how to manage them.

Listed below are some typical employee profiles. Take a few moments to write down what kind of goals these people are likely to have and what course of action you can take to meet their needs.

Employee Characteristics	Most Likely Goals	Best Course of Action
1. Likes routine, seeks constant approval.	_____	_____
2. Values duty and loyalty, strong work ethic.	_____	_____
3. Controlling and manipulating.	_____	_____
4. Likes working with other people.	_____	_____
5. Looks for challenges and new things to do.	_____	_____
6. Likes to work alone.	_____	_____

ESTABLISHING AND EXERCISING AUTHORITY

The power of leadership—*authority*—is derived in three basic ways:

1. Situations occur that require leadership, and through a general consensus, one individual earns that recognition from the group. The leader assumes control.

2. Specific activities or projects require a leader—often the person with the most skill or experience. Skill or experience is frequently a factor in the promotion of a new supervisor.

3. The title or position demands respect and recognition. In a small business, for example, it is rare for anyone to outrank the title of "owner." Titles can provide leadership, but they don't guarantee that the leader has any leadership skills.

If you depend on your position or authority alone, you're likely to see a high turnover in your work force and a lack of productivity. Durable and solid leadership can be established through a combination of methods. A true leader is a person who people want to follow because they trust and respect that individual.

Based on the broad skills outlined in this chapter, list leadership skills you need to work on:

_____

_____

_____

_____

_____

_____

_____

Chart your progress, check this list again when you've completed the book, and plan to spend more time on any areas that you still feel are weak. That time may include additional reading or training.

Chapter Checkpoints

✓ Do you have confidence in your ability to be a supervisor?

✓ Can you communicate clearly?

✓ Are you comfortable making decisions and sticking with them?

✓ Do you take pride in developing the skills of others?

✓ Do you feel your subordinates respect you and follow your direction?

3 | Decision Making

This chapter will help you to:

- Learn to approach a decision with an open mind.
- Use a decision planner to evaluate the likely results of a decision.
- Prepare to "sell" decisions to the people they affect.

As shift supervisor at a large bakery, Joan is faced with many decisions on a daily basis. These decisions range from scheduling her employees' hours and determining their work assignments to participating in the quality committee with other supervisors and making suggestions for plant operations. Joan is irritated by having to settle what she feels are minor disputes between employees, particularly in the area of work assignments. It seems that whatever she does, someone is unhappy with her decision. She often feels it would be easier just to ignore these disputes and hope the problems go away. ■

FOCUS ON DECISIONS

Decision making is an essential part of any supervisory job. Many executives consider it their primary responsibility.

Decision making is also one of the most difficult tasks for many new supervisors. When you were a first-line employee, you had decisions made for you. Policy and direction of work were not your major concern.

As a supervisor, however, the situation is different:

- *Decision making is an essential part of supervising others.* Be

3

careful to not trivialize decisions that may be of great importance to your employees.

- *Not all your decisions will be the right ones.* Everyone makes mistakes, including CEOs of large companies.

- *Failing to take any action at all is also a decision.* Deciding not to decide carries the same risks and rewards as any other decision.

KEEP AN OPEN MIND

How do you make good decisions as often as possible? Good decisions result from collecting information. Be informed.

Five key steps to approaching a decision are:

1. *Be truly open-minded.* Don't take sides or make judgments until you can examine all the information. Be aware that in many cases, you will be required to make a decision without complete information. Make the best possible decision with as much information as you can get.

2. *Avoid taking sides.* Don't assume that because one side in a dispute has a better track record than the other, that side will always be right. Taking sides is not only unfair to everyone involved, but it can often lead to a poor decision.

3. *Recognize your own bias.* What seems obvious to you as a supervisor may not be obvious to your employees. Your perspective is different. If we all saw things the same way, there would be no disputes or issues to resolve. The reality is that "obvious truths" are only obvious to those who believe them to be true.

4. *Don't let titles or prestige influence your decision.* An individual's title may not be indicative of a person's skill or experience. Decisions must be made on the merit of the situation, not the title or image of the people involved.

5. *Avoid "absolute" wording in your decision.* Words such as *always* or *never* should be avoided. Rarely are situations that permanent. Qualify the conditions that affect your decisions.

Ask yourself these four critical questions as you set out to make a decision:

- Do I have enough information to make a decision?
- Does the problem require a decision?
- Am I the best person to make this decision?
- What will be the worst possible result if I make an incorrect decision?

Describe a decision (large or small) that you are currently facing: ___

_____

_____

_____

Ask yourself the four critical questions above. Jot down your answers here: _____

_____

_____

_____

EVALUATE THE DECISION

Decisions are not made in a vacuum. Each decision you make carries implications for other people and future decisions. Below is a decision planner to help you chart the impact that your decisions will have on the future. Eventually, this process can become part of every decision you make.

Decision Planner

Problem/Decision Issues

Clearly stated and defined: _____

_____

_____

Long-Range Effects:

How long will/should the decision be in effect? Can it be changed or reversed if necessary? What are the most likely results of the decision?

1.

2.

3.

What is the worst-case scenario that could result?

_____

_____

Is the worst-case scenario acceptable?

Effects on Others

Who else will be affected by the decision? Who else should be involved in making the decision?

	Affected by Decision	Involved in Decision
Number/names of employees		
Other supervisors		

Managers/my department

Managers/supervisors in
other departments

_____

Who else should be informed of the decision?

_____
_____

Company Policy and Procedures

Does the decision contradict or change current company policy?
Is the decision in the tradition of other decisions made previously by
the company? Does the decision fit the style and philosophy of the
company, or is it likely to be opposed? Do you and/or the company
have whatever resources are needed to implement the decision?

What will the financial impact of the decision be?

_____
_____

Who will be designated to carry out the decision? _____

_____

Uniqueness of the Problem

Is the problem truly unique and not addressed by other company
policies and procedures? _____

_____

Is the situation likely to occur again, requiring longer-range
thinking? _____

_____

Is the decision creating new company policy? _____

_____
_____
_____

THE DECISION-MAKING PROCESS

In any decision, you have three options:

1. Proceed (yes).

3

2. Should it be in writing, and, if so, how should I organize the information?

3. Is my presentation of the decision phrased in language that will gain support for the decision?

4. What negative responses might I expect?

5. When and how will the information be presented to the employees involved?

6. What questions are likely to come from superiors and employees when I present the decision?

The timing and method of presenting your ideas can make a great deal of difference. Think about the best time and method to present your decision. In your company, is new information usually presented in formal memos, all-desk announcements, or in one-on-one conversations? Depending on the situation, does the decision need to be delivered to everyone, or just the individuals involved?

Think about a decision you'll soon have to make, or one that you've made recently, and what you'll need to do to gain acceptance for it. Ask yourself the six key questions above and jot your answers here: _____

_____

_____

_____

_____

_____

Chapter Checkpoints

✓ Have you defined your decision?

✓ Have you analyzed the problem to eliminate bias and maintain an open mind?

✓ Who else will be affected by the decision?

✓ Does the decision have ramifications for other policies and procedures?

✓ Is the decision consistent with company policy and procedures?

✓ Do you have the resources to implement the decision you want to make?

✓ Have you prepared whatever is necessary to sell your decision to the affected individuals?

CHAPTER

4 | Managing Change

This chapter will help you to:

- Acknowledge the difficulty of accepting change.
- Learn how to implement change.
- Recognize the importance of promoting the need for change.

Don is an office manager for a prestigious law firm. His company is growing rapidly—adding new people and offering new services. As a result of this growth, combined with ever-changing government regulations affecting his company's policies and procedures, Don feels as if he's in a constant state of change.

Every time Don's company designs new forms or methods, they seem to be out of date. A constant blizzard of paperwork affects Don and everyone in his department. There are always new ways to do things and new forms to complete. Several valuable employees have left in frustration. ■

ACCEPTING CHANGE

Change is inevitable. What worked in the past or, for that matter, what works today may not work tomorrow.

Change is one of the most difficult aspects of business—or life—for many people to accept. By nature, most humans seek consistency and familiarity. The majority of people are not risk-takers or adventurers, so change is uncomfortable.

Each time change occurs, our confidence level drops. After finally perfecting a task, or accepting an idea, we have to start all over again.

4

Review your goals and objectives from Chapter 1. As you'll see below, change can have a direct impact on goals.

IMPLEMENTING CHANGE

Changes can and will occur in technology, legislation, societal attitudes and mores, personal wants and needs, management and supervisory techniques, company–employee relationships, and virtually every other situation we face on a daily basis. For example, look at today's office. Fax machines, computers, portable cellular phones and elaborate telephone systems were uncommon just a few years ago. Change is likely to accelerate at an even faster rate in the future.

So much change creates a great challenge for supervisors. You must continually sell the need for change to your employees, in addition to accepting it personally.

The Impact of Change on My Goals

1. Personal Goals—Long Range and Short Range

List the assumptions around which you built your plans. For example, if one of your objectives is to buy a new car, what assumptions are you making about events beyond your control? Getting an annual raise, avoiding emergencies that could eat into your cash reserves, or feeling assured your rent will not increase are some influences beyond your control.

Personal Goal	Noncontrollable Events that Could Affect the Goal
_____	_____
_____	_____
_____	_____
_____	_____
_____	_____

2. Business Goals

Repeat the process with your business goals.

Goals	Events
_____	_____
_____	_____
_____	_____
_____	_____
_____	_____

When implementing change:

1. Make a Decision and Stick to It

Review the facts and whatever information you've collected and commit to the change you believe should be made.

2. Develop a Plan

Decide on a plan to sell the new methods or new techniques to those employees who will be directly involved.

3. Plan Each Phase of the Change

For example, in Chapter 3, Joan decided to shift an employee from one department to another in the bakery. That change needs to be thought through with a plan to anticipate and cover each step.

In our decision planner in Chapter 3, Joan would probably want to include the following:

- Explain to Jim the reasons for the change.
- Explain to Jim's new supervisor why the change is occurring.
- Have the new supervisor explain any new tasks Jim needs to learn.
- Explain to the other employees how the change will affect their jobs and discuss any future plans regarding personnel.

4. Examine Possible Alternatives to Each Step; Draw Up Contingency Plans

Using the decision planner from Chapter 3, anticipate what would happen if Jim hated the new job. Joan needs a contingency plan. She might want to talk to her manager and see what other options would be open for Jim if the transfer doesn't work out. She could put Jim back in his original job and move Sally instead, or find some method to help them get along.

5. Monitor Employee Behavior to Ensure the Changes Are Implemented

Here's an example.

Don, the supervisor in the law firm, is regularly faced with a barrage of changes. One change that the law firm institutes is a new compensation program that rewards employees for their productivity. At the same time, their base pay is reduced, with the potential for top employees to earn more.

A likely outcome is that Don will find some employees excited about the new plan, others taking a wait-and-see attitude, and still others ready to sabotage the plan or quit their jobs. Their behavior and reactions will be Don's most visible clues.

The reality is that Don may lose some employees to frustration and a sense of loss. At the same time, other employees may become more valuable and more loyal.

Here's an example of how Don might monitor employee behavior resulting from the change described above:

Behavior change: The goal is for each employee to process two more invoices per hour.

Employees	*Date: Week One*
Esther	*Handling one more per hour*
Charles	*No change*
Kathy	*Doing one less per hour*

6. Accept and Plan for the Results of Change

It's quite possible that the new ideas and methods you implement will result in work reassignments, changes in personnel, or new tasks. As a supervisor you should think of the possible outcomes and the likely results.

Change Implementation Plan

Select a decision you are currently facing and develop a change implementation plan using the steps we've outlined.

1. Decision
Describe the decision you must make or have made.

_____

_____

_____

_____

2. Describe Your Method of Introducing and Selling It to Your Employees
More information on this will follow.

_____

_____

_____

_____

(*continued*)

3. Break Your Change Down into Smaller Steps

We did this in our examples.

_____

_____

_____

_____

_____

4. Create a Contingency Plan

Possible Problem Result	Contingency Plan
_____	_____
_____	_____
_____	_____
_____	_____
_____	_____

5. Monitor Your Employees' Implementation of the Change

List the behavior changes required and, under each behavior, list each employee's response. Monitor behavior over the time period you've allowed for the change.

_____

_____

_____

_____

6. Accept and Plan for the Results of Change

At the end of the acceptable break-in period, list the actions you plan to take for those who aren't meeting objectives.

_____

_____

_____

_____

_____

PROMOTING THE NEED FOR CHANGE

Being committed to a change and getting others to accept it are two different things. A planned change may result from outside influences, as in Don's situation. It may also result from you or one of your employees finding a better way to do things. In either case, you'll probably need to sell this change.

New ideas from your superiors may have to be sold to employees. New ideas from you or your staff may have to be sold to your superiors. In both cases, clearly define the change and list the benefits—how the change will help the company and the employees.

To sell a change to employees, follow these steps:

1. Present the new idea to employees in clear, accessible language, both verbally and in writing. Include the reasons for the change. It's much easier to get an idea accepted if people know why the change is occurring. For example, Don (the law office supervisor) might explain to his employees the need for another new form because of a new government regulation. He could then explain the reasons and goals for the new regulation.

2. Present your ideas in positive, sales-oriented language, even if the change is likely to be resisted. Put it in the most positive light possible.

3. As the new change is implemented, stress your willingness to help employees adapt. Be supportive as problems occur.

4. If the change is a major one, ask each employee to tell you how he or she plans to handle it on the job. Let your employees know you're personally interested in helping them.

5. If the change has other unintended results, be open to reviewing what has occurred and to responding as needed.

To sell your ideas for change to your superiors, you'll need to follow steps 1 and 2. As with employees, present your ideas in clear, easy-to-understand language, both verbally and in writing. Use positive, sales-oriented language. After that, you must await their decision.

To influence that decision, be prepared to provide additional supportive information and even to negotiate on some points of your new plan.

Don't be afraid to offer new ideas. Most company managers welcome new methods and creativity on the part of their employees and supervisors.

Chapter Checkpoints

✓ Are you open to new ideas and change?

✓ In your own personal plans, have you taken into account external situations you can't control? Have you listed these factors that can affect your plans?

✓ Have you developed contingency plans?

✓ Do you take the time to sell the benefits of your ideas?

✓ Do you plan ways to implement change with minimal disruption?

5 | Managing Your Time

This chapter will help you to:

- Identify your major time-wasters.
- Prioritize your work.
- Debunk some common myths that affect time management.

Parkinson's first law:

Work expands to fill the time.

Parkinson's second law:

Managers (and supervisors) tend to spend time amounts inversely related to the importance of their tasks.

C. Northcote Parkinson

Do you find your workload overwhelming? Does it feel like you're always behind on the projects you need to handle? Are things falling through the cracks and not getting done? Is your workday getting longer with no major improvement in results? ∎

GETTING CONTROL

Loss of control over your time creates these uncomfortable feelings. As a supervisor, you get tugged in all directions by people bringing what often seems like a never-ending stream of urgent problems.

What can you do? The first step is to determine that you *want* to control your time. Doing so will most likely involve delegating work to a greater degree (see Chapter 9), but you can also take more time, now, to solve

5

your time problems. You'll learn to carefully manage your long-term projects as well as address the day-to-day issues that come up.

Although this chapter will give you immediate tips on time management, consider reading more on the subject on your own after you've completed this chapter.

IDENTIFYING MAJOR TIME–WASTERS

What are the most common time-wasters? The box below lists the most common time-wasters. Do any of these sound familiar?

Time-Wasters

Rate yourself on managing each time-waster, from excellent (give yourself a 1) to average (give yourself a 2) to need help (give yourself a 3).

Time-Waster	**My Rating**
1. No priorities on my work	____
2. Doing too many things at once; leaving tasks unfinished	____
3. Too much attention to detail of other people's work	____
4. Too many meetings	____
5. Meetings run too long	____
6. Procrastination	____
7. Solving employees' personal problems	____
8. Long phone conversations	____
9. Doing my employees' work	____
10. Unrealistic time estimates of projects	____
11. Poor scheduling	____
12. Poor communication with employees	____
13. Poor communication with superiors	____
14. Too much paperwork with no clearly identified need	____

5

An ideal score is 14, of course. A score of 22 or more indicates a need for improvement. A score of 28 or more means you probably feel like you're drowning. You need to make a conscious decision to manage your time more effectively.

How did you do? What areas can you address? There are likely a few areas where you know how to solve the problem. If possible, eliminate the issues that turn daily tasks into time-wasters. For instance, you may be able to easily cut back on long phone calls or make a point of only attending those meetings requiring your attendance. Can you identify your top five time-wasters?

For many new supervisors, setting priorities is the most difficult aspect of time management. The next section addresses this tricky problem.

PRIORITIZING YOUR WORK

Not all projects and needs are equal. Part of your job as a supervisor is to make decisions (see Chapter 3) and determine what projects are most important and need your attention first.

In Chapter 3, we discussed the need for getting as much information as possible to make the best possible decision. The same advice holds true for time management.

Use the time log below for one workday. Adjust the hours as needed and keep a record of your activities in 15-minute increments as shown. Duplicate 14 copies of this time log and track your time for two weeks. You may be surprised at how you really spend your time.

Time Log

Task	Could Be Delegated?*	
	Yes	No
8:00–8:15		
8:15–8:30		
8:30–8:45		
8:45–9:00		
9:00–9:15		
9:15–9:30		
9:30–9:45		
9:45–10:00		
10:00–10:15		
10:15–10:30		
10:30–10:45		
10:45–11:00		

11:00–11:15	_____	_____	_____
11:15–11:30	_____	_____	_____
11:30–11:45	_____	_____	_____
11:45–12:00	_____	_____	_____
Lunch			
1:00–1:15	_____	_____	_____
1:15–1:30	_____	_____	_____
1:30–1:45	_____	_____	_____
1:45–2:00	_____	_____	_____
2:00–2:15	_____	_____	_____
2:15–2:30	_____	_____	_____
2:30–2:45	_____	_____	_____
2:45–3:00	_____	_____	_____
3:00–3:15	_____	_____	_____
3:15–3:30	_____	_____	_____
3:30–3:45	_____	_____	_____
3:45–4:00	_____	_____	_____
4:00–4:15	_____	_____	_____
4:15–4:30	_____	_____	_____
4:30–4:45	_____	_____	_____
4:45–5:00	_____	_____	_____

* Be honest in your appraisal. Don't worry about who else could handle the task yet, only whether it could be handled by someone else.

How did you do on the first day of filling in the log? Frequently, supervisors find they spend more time on projects they thought took little time (perhaps because the projects are more interesting, enjoyable, or easier) and actually very little time on projects that seem to be all-consuming (because the projects may be boring or difficult).

Before you can build a priority plan, you must know how you really spend your time. Doing this chart for a minimum of one week is essential. Two weeks of record-keeping will give you more accurate information.

CREATING YOUR OWN PRIORITY PLAN

In the space provided below, list all the activities that showed up on your time log. Next to each one, put:

1 For an activity that you yourself must absolutely do.

2 For an activity that you really should do.

3 For an activity that you'd like to do but don't really need to do yourself.

Next to each task or activity, you should also list how much time per week you spend on it.

When you've completed the list, total up the time spent for number 1 tasks, number 2 tasks, and number 3 tasks. Then, assuming you work a 40-hour week, start eliminating number 3 tasks first, followed by number 2 tasks that put you over your available time. You can eliminate tasks through a combination of delegation (see Chapter 9) and better management of each task in your number 1 and number 2 categories.

Priority Plan

Activity or Task	Priority	Time Spent
_____	_____	_____
_____	_____	_____
_____	_____	_____
_____	_____	_____
_____	_____	_____
_____	_____	_____
_____	_____	_____
_____	_____	_____
_____	_____	_____
_____	_____	_____

_____   _____   _____
_____   _____   _____
_____   _____   _____
_____   _____   _____
_____   _____   _____
_____   _____   _____
_____   _____   _____
_____   _____   _____
_____   _____   _____
_____   _____   _____
_____   _____   _____
_____   _____   _____

5

To improve your time management, try the following proven steps:

1. *Make weekly and daily to-do lists in order of priority.* Check off each task as it's completed, and you'll feel far more accomplished at the end of the day.

2. *Plan what you're going to do at least one day ahead.* If you know what tasks await you tomorrow, organize *tomorrow's* to-do list today!

3. *Plan telephone calls in advance.* By doing this, you know what you want to cover and can reduce your time on the phone.

4. *Plan meetings (one-on-one or with a group) in advance.* If you call the meeting, take control of the agenda and stay on the subject.

5. *Evaluate your time management several times during the day.* Take a look at how you're doing about one third of the way through your workday and again about two thirds of the way through. Will you meet your objectives for the day? If not, what got in the way? Should it take precedence over what you planned to do? Emergencies do come up and must be dealt with. Your priorities may change in these situations.

6. *Look at your personal list of major time-wasters.* Develop an action plan to do something about your worst offenders.

DEBUNKING SOME COMMON MYTHS

Myth 1: Being Busy Is Being Productive

Not if you're spending your time on number 3 priorities or fun tasks that don't really help you as a supervisor. Being busy has nothing to do with productivity. Maximizing how you use your time means a great deal more. It will open either more free time for you or more time for creating new ideas.

Myth 2: Efficiency Is Effectiveness

Only if your efficiency is in the right tasks. New supervisors often find themselves highly efficient at their old jobs and far less efficient at being a supervisor. It's more important to jump in with both feet and tackle the tasks of supervision than to continue to improve your efficiency in the old job.

Myth 3: An Open-Door Policy Works Best

There's no question that employees who have access to their bosses on a regular basis are happier and more productive. Unfortunately, as a supervisor, you must place some limits on the use of your time. It is essential to preserve time for yourself to handle the supportive tasks of supervision as well as the face-to-face tasks. Consider specifying regular times when you're available and times when you're not to be disturbed.

Chapter Checkpoints

✓ Do you consciously want to get better control of your time?

✓ Have you identified your personal top five time-wasters?

✓ Do you know how you actually spend your time?

✓ Have you prioritized your tasks?

✓ Have you determined what you can realistically accomplish?

✓ Do you prepare a daily to-do list?

✓ Do you take time to evaluate your progress several times a day against your to-do list?

6 | Communicating Effectively

This chapter will help you to:

- Listen effectively.
- Consider the meaning of body language.
- Get yourself heard.
- Use a checklist for good written communication.

Sandra is a supervisor in a food-processing plant that belongs to a large retail grocery chain. Her plant produces store brand products for the retail stores. She is younger and better educated than many of her employees and feels that she has great difficulty getting the support of her staff. They just don't seem to pay attention to her, and they complain that she really doesn't understand them or their needs. In her mind, there's a real "people problem," and she feels at a loss to solve it. ■

"PEOPLE PROBLEMS" ARE OFTEN COMMUNICATION PROBLEMS

Problems like Sandra's are often communication problems. Age, gender, education, cultural background, and a host of other factors can create communication gaps. The root of many problems is often a failure to communicate in a common language.

As a supervisor, you'll need to recognize those differences and develop a communication style that will help you reach each person. In any society, words and gestures often mean different things to different people. Understanding these differences is a valuable skill for a new supervisor.

HOW TO LISTEN EFFECTIVELY

Communication is always a two-way process. Someone says something
. . . and someone else hears what was said. Since each person comes to
the listening situation with different backgrounds, there is often a gap
between the speaker's intention and the listener's interpretation.

Ineffective listening can be a major communication problem. As a
supervisor who listens carefully, you'll have fewer people problems and
more career success.

The Listening Process

The background and experience of each listener influences what is heard.
If the experiences of speaker and listener are entirely different, there may
be no communication.

Says words

Speaker formulates idea

Words heard

Meaning of words interpreted

6

Some years ago, an experiment with school children was carried out to analyze the kinds of words that were easiest to learn to spell. Conventional wisdom had always held that shorter words were easier to learn. The results showed that nouns were easier to spell than adjectives, even though adjectives (this, blue, big) were often shorter. Why? Nouns have tangible meaning, so people can picture them, thus making them easier to spell.

But there was a catch: nouns were easy to spell only if the nouns were familiar. For example, the word cactus was easy for students in the southwest. It was more difficult for students elsewhere who had never seen a cactus.

Everybody understands concepts in the context of their own backgrounds. As a supervisor, you must be aware of your own background and prejudices and try to eliminate them when you communicate with others.

Think of someone with whom you have trouble communicating. Write down what you know about that person's background (age, gender, education, cultural background, and so on). Then, compare this information with your own background.

_____

_____

_____

_____

Do you think that differences in background are the source of your problem?

_____

_____

_____

_____

Here are seven key steps to effective listening.

1. *Ask questions.* If something is unclear or seems to contradict what fits your own personal sense of logic, ask questions. Asking questions shows that you're interested in understanding what's being said.

2. *Concentrate.* Don't let your mind wander. People think at the rate of about 500 words per mintue, but people talk at a rate of only about 150 words per minute. Stay focused on what is being said, or you risk missing key points.

3. *Listen for the main idea(s).* It's not uncommon for people to formulate ideas as they talk, to be somewhat vague when discussing sensitive issues, or to have trouble coming to the point. Make sure you determine what their key issues are. Restate the other person's main ideas in your own words and ask if you've understood correctly.

4. *Listen for the rationale behind what the other person is saying.* This is especially important if what they're saying doesn't seem to make sense to you. An employee may be making a request on the basis of erroneous information about the company. Be sensitive and make sure you understand *why* people say what they do.

5. *Listen for key words.* Key words can become your own internal cue or memory stimulator to help you retain what you hear.

6. *Organize what you hear in your own mind in a way that is logical for you.* Your way of organizing information may differ from the way the information was presented, but it is critical for you to use what you hear.

7. *Take notes if the issue or request is complex.* It's worth getting your thoughts down in writing.

Think again about the person you described in the previous exercise. Which of the seven steps that we've just discussed might help you listen more effectively to that person? _____

_____

_____

_____

_____

Try using the techniques you've selected the next time you talk with this person. Did they help you listen?

A BRIEF PRIMER ON BODY LANGUAGE

Your verbal language conveys only part of what you mean. Body language—your gestures and movements—says the rest. The meanings of gestures and movements vary greatly from culture to culture. Here are just a few of the most common gestures in the United States and what they generally mean. Remember, in today's multicultural work force, some of these gestures will have different meanings in different cultures. Check your library or bookstore for references on body language in various cultures.

- Leaning forward is a positive gesture. The person is listening carefully and wants to hear what is said.
- Direct eye contact is a positive gesture. Again, recognize this as a U.S. trait. Many Asian societies find direct eye contact quite rude.
- Open hands are a sign of agreement and careful listening.
- Arms folded over the chest is usually a very negative sign. Your words probably aren't getting through.
- Leaning away from you in a chair may indicate disinterest in what you are saying.
- Backing away or avoidance is generally a sign of disagreement with what you say.

Be aware of the gestures your employees and managers make as well as the signals you send with the same gestures.

Think once again about your face-to-face communication with the person in the previous exercises. What do you recall about that person's body language? About your own body language? _____

_____

_____

_____

_____

What body language might you use to improve your communications with this person? _____

_____

_____

_____

_____

6

HOW TO GET YOURSELF HEARD

How can you get yourself heard? Here are nine basic steps to help get your message out.

1. *Present one idea at a time.* For example, if you're training employees in a new process, break the process down into its most basic steps. Present each step separately and make sure the step is understood before going on. If possible, provide an example or illustration of what you're trying to say to help overcome any built-in listening bias.

2. *Keep it simple.* Use basic language with common use words. The English language is ambiguous enough without using slang, jargon, industry buzzwords, and so on.

3. *Make it brief.* Don't take more words or time than needed. Rather than clarify, highly detailed explanations may create confusion.

4. *Personalize what you're saying and present it to the individual.* Avoid generalizing or sounding vague. Add a personal touch.

5. *Use the right tone of voice and the right body language for the situation.* Make sure your voice and body language match the message you want to send. It seems obvious, but be aware of how you sound and look. Sounding bored or looking disinterested tells the person you're talking to that what you're saying is not important.

6. *Get acceptance of each idea you present.* Make sure the person understands you. If the person looks confused or doesn't question your ideas, he or she may not clearly understand what you said. Ask if anything needs clearing up before you go on to your next point.

7. *Respond to the emotions of the people with whom you're talking.* Many times the subject will generate strong feelings. Watch body language and listen carefully to what people say.

8. *Appreciate your listeners' concerns.* Your listeners may disagree with you, in which case it's important to find out the basis of that disagreement. You don't have to back down from your position, just be sensitive to your listeners' reactions.

9. *Encourage your listeners to express themselves.* Welcome their thoughts and ideas so you'll know how they're reacting. Again, you don't have to agree, but it's important for you to know what others are thinking.

Think about the last time you spoke to a group of your employees. Which of the nine steps above did you use?

_____

_____

_____

_____

Plan your next communication with a group of your employees. Which of the nine steps will be particularly helpful to you?_____

_____

_____

_____

EFFECTIVE WRITING

Read the following memo from Sandra to her staff in the food-processing plant, then answer the questions that follow. They make up a checklist of the basics of good written communication.

MEMO

To All Department Employees:
Your Good Ideas Can Mean More Money in Your Pocket

Our company is launching a new suggestion award program that is open to all employees.

Based on the idea that you know better than anyone else (including supervisors and managers) what we do well and where we need to improve, the company is offering a reward for every good suggestion made to improve the way we do things.

Submit each suggestion to me on the attached form (I have more copies of the form if you need them). I will pass all suggestions on to our suggestion review committee. The committee consists of one frontline employee and one supervisor from each department.

The committee will evaluate your suggestion, and you will earn an award based on what we feel your suggestion will contribute to the company's growth and well-being. An award schedule is also attached.

Please review the following documents and call or see me if you have any questions.

CHECKLIST FOR GOOD WRITTEN COMMUNICATION

☐ Does it command the reader's attention?

☐ Does it arouse interest in the reader?

☐ Does it get the reader involved?

☐ Does it get the reader to take action (promising a benefit, providing proof of the need for something, communicating a sense of urgency, and so on)?

☐ Is it reader oriented rather than writer oriented?

☐ Is it clear and concise?

☐ Is it tactful and courteous (no threatening language)?

☐ Is the tone conversational and the English simple?

☐ Is the information useful to the reader?

☐ Is it likely to produce the desired impact on the reader?

When you put something in writing, compare it to this checklist to make sure it sends the message you want to send. If not, revise your communication to clarify your message and make it more effective.

6

Chapter Checkpoints

✓ Do you listen carefully to others?

✓ Are you sensitive to cultural, educational, generational, and gender differences in the people you talk with?

✓ Do you recognize your own biases and try to set them aside?

✓ Do you present your ideas clearly and in simple language?

✓ Are you sensitive to the reactions you get from others, both verbal and nonverbal (body language)?

✓ Do you write clearly and in a reader-oriented manner?

7 | Making Meetings Productive

This chapter will help you to:

- Prepare for one-on-one meetings with an employee or manager.
- Run your own meeting with a group.
- Address typical meeting problems.

Omar was recently promoted to supervisor in a customer service center for a major bank. He has participated in meetings on quality, customer care, office procedures, and, of course, he has had one-to-one conferences with his supervisor. Now he's the one running meetings, and there are a lot of them. He participates in a weekly meeting for supervisors, as well as weekly meetings with his staff where he has to create the agenda and run the meeting.

In addition, there seems to be a never-ending stream of meetings with his employees, his associates, people from other departments, customers, and suppliers. ■

ONE-ON-ONE MEETINGS

As a supervisor, the one-on-one meeting is the most common type you will experience. This type includes meetings with your staff, your manager, other management personnel, other supervisors, customers or clients, suppliers, and sometimes prospective customers or suppliers.

If you initiate the meeting, prepare to maximize its effectiveness. Start by rereading Chapters 5 and 6 on time management and effective communication. Then ask yourself the following questions. Don't begin your meeting until you have answers.

7

1. What is the purpose of this meeting?
2. How long should it take?
3. What am I going to say, and in what order?
4. What is the outcome I want? What am I expecting the other person to do?
5. What reactions are likely to what I'm going to say?
6. What other topics are likely to come up, and am I prepared for them?
7. What is my reason to end the meeting when I'm done?

Before going into your next one-on-one meeting, complete the following form.

One-on-One Meeting Preparation Form

Meeting with _____

Purposes _____

_____

_____

Desired result _____

_____

_____

Key points I'm going to make
1. _____
2. _____
3. _____

Likely Response	**My Reply**
_____	_____
_____	_____
_____	_____
_____	_____

Results of the meeting _____

_____

_____

Action to be taken

By me _____

By _____

_____

_____

7

WHEN SOMEONE ELSE CALLS THE MEETING

If your superior calls the meeting, you cannot do much to control the agenda, but you can certainly take steps to be as prepared as possible.

Preparing might include researching information that your manager might request, creating a report, or being aware of a particular situation.

If someone on your staff calls the meeting, you should take similar steps. You do retain the right to control the agenda if you think the employee's agenda is inappropriate. Out of courtesy, you should offer your employees a chance to present their thoughts and ideas in one-on-one meetings without feeling threatened or constrained. The flow of accurate information is critical to you, your manager, and your employees. You should not do anything to discourage people from being open and honest with you.

LEADING A MEETING WITH YOUR GROUP

Supervisor-led meetings are a mainstay of business. They cover everything from presenting company policy to hearing employee problems, from developing quality methods to reviewing processes and procedures.

If you've sat through meetings that were boring, that didn't affect you, or that you didn't care about, follow the steps outlined below to make your meetings better.

1. *Avoid a meeting, if possible.* Step 1 is not a contradiction. If you can convey the same information by memo or on the phone with each person, it will probably be faster. Meetings are one of the biggest time-wasters in business today. You may have indicated meetings on one of your top five time-wasters in Chapter 5.

2. *Keep the group small.* Smaller groups tend to work more effectively and rapidly. You'll get more interaction as well, since attendees are more willing to speak up in smaller groups.
   If your group will be voting on issues, have an odd number of people to avoid ties. You want *decisions* on issues or ideas, not plans for another meeting.

3. *Give everyone an agenda in advance.* Tell everyone what will be covered, and let everyone know that only items on the agenda will be discussed. If you want to allow people to add their own ideas, that's fine—but again, the complete agenda should go out to everyone in advance.
   Word your agenda carefully to describe the issues in broad terms without imposing a decision. For example, suppose Omar,

our bank customer service supervisor, were to include on a staff meeting agenda, "Improving the telephone system to speed up customer response." What kind of reaction would he get? Omar is already assuming the telephone system is the problem when, in fact, other issues may pose problems as well. Omar will have limited everyone to talking about the phone system as the only issue when, in fact, it may not be the cause of the problem.

4. *Invite only those people who really need to attend.* Sometimes protocol requires inviting certain people but, if possible, stick with rule 2 (keep the group small).

5. *Start on time and end as soon as you've covered your agenda.* Don't get into other subject areas, and don't delay your starting time. Attendees should be ready when the meeting is scheduled.

6. *Keep the discussion focused.* Don't let participants get off on tangents or other issues. Save those for future meetings. One way to bring the discussion back to where you want it is to ask a question related to the subject. If Omar was discussing customer service response and someone got off track discussing the different telephone systems available, Omar could ask the group, "What other steps besides an improved telephone system would help us improve customer response?"

7. *When someone suggests an idea, write it down and repeat it with slightly different phrasing.* The objective is to get the whole group involved with the idea, not just the individual who presented it.

8. *If someone criticizes someone else in the group, jump in immediately and rephrase their comment in a more positive way.* You don't want your meeting to become a personal gripe session. For example, if Marta complains, "Carlos, you're so inexperienced that you can't see beyond the problems with the telephone system!", Omar might rephrase and redirect the comment by saying, "Marta thinks we may have other problems besides the telephone system. What other problems do we have?"

9. *Draw in everyone.* Assuming everyone has a reason to be there, ask questions or opinions from the quiet attendees. Make them a part of the discussion.

10. *Don't be afraid of heated discussion or disagreement, as long as it doesn't involve personal attacks.* Some new ideas may result, and you want to encourage people to express what they're thinking.

11. *Remain calm and neutral, whatever happens.* Your role as a supervisor is to moderate and facilitate, not to take sides or discourage comments.

Follow these 11 steps, and you're on your way to running productive meetings that are worth the time and effort of everyone involved.

Think about the last meeting you ran, or pick one that you recently attended. Which of the 11 steps might have improved the meeting? ___

_____
_____
_____
_____

TYPICAL MEETING PROBLEMS

When you're running a meeting, it's up to you to keep the meeting on track. You need to deal quickly with problems that arise so they won't derail your meeting. Most typical meeting problems can be handled simply and effectively, as outlined in the following tips.

Problem	Response
One or two people dominate the discussion	Set a time limit on each response
One or two won't talk	Ask them for an opinion
People are losing interest	Ask someone in the group for a specific example or move to another subject
Discussion drifts off the subject	Ask questions to get them back on the topic
An argument develops	Remind the group that it's okay for people to have different opinions, and encourage everyone to hear both points of view
You make an obvious mistake	Admit it and joke about it—supervisors aren't expected to be perfect

Note typical meeting problems that are common in meetings at your workplace. _____

_____
_____
_____

When you're running a meeting, or even when you're just participating, try the responses we've suggested when problems develop. What effect does the response have? _____

_____

_____

Meetings with productive outcomes are greatly influenced by how you manage the meeting. If you follow the 11 steps and move quickly to handle problems, you'll need far fewer meetings and get better results from the meetings that you do have.

7

Chapter Checkpoints

For One-on-One Meetings that You Set Up, Do You

✓ Think in advance about what you're going to say and how you will say it?

✓ Anticipate how you might reply to the other person's response?

For One-on-One Meetings Called by Others, Do You

✓ Think about what information you'll need to prepare?

✓ Ask in advance what the purpose of the meeting is?

For Group Meetings that You Run, Do You

✓ Prepare in advance, involve everyone, and provide an open environment for discussion?

8 | Praise, Criticism, and Conflict

This chapter will help you to:

- Learn how and when praise should be used.
- Learn how and when criticism should be used.
- Manage employee conflicts.

Kelly recently started as a nursing supervisor at a large hospital in a major city. Her predecessor left several months prior to her arrival, and the staff has been reporting directly to her manager. Because there has been no direct supervision for several months, Kelly is finding it necessary to talk to her staff and get things in shape. Some of them have been doing a great job, while others have been well below acceptable levels. A number of unresolved conflicts also remain undecided. ■

USING PRAISE

Praise is a powerful tool for any supervisor. As you recall from Chapter 2, it ranks very high on the list of what people want from their jobs. Your staff wants to be recognized when they do something well or something beyond their basic responsibilities. This recognition reaffirms their own self-worth and increases their confidence in doing a good job.

When using praise:

- *Mean what you say.* Make it sincere. Don't exaggerate or say things you don't really mean, as it diminishes the impact of the praise.
- *Say what you mean.* Don't "pile it on." Be specific and avoid generalities like "great job." Kelly's employees would rather hear

8

"you did an excellent job of handling the rush of patients we had in the emergency room today."

- *Balance your use.* Praise, while a great form of recognition, will lose most of its impact if it becomes regular and predictable. If every effort earns high praise, any praise will mean nothing in a very short period of time. Save it for when it's deserved.

- *Use praise to provide encouragement.* If you ask one of your staff to take on a new assignment, use praise to express your confidence in them to get the job done. After they've accomplished the task, they'll have more self-confidence. Up front, it may be very helpful to them.

Think about the times you've been praised by your supervisor or manager. Make a note of how that person praised you, and how you felt as a result. _____

_____

_____

_____

_____

When Is the Best Time to Praise People?

The best time is right after they've completed a task or when they're ready to take on new and challenging work.

Praise offered soon after a task has great influence for several reasons:

- The task is fresh in the mind of your employee.
- You demonstrated your interest in what they were doing soon after it was completed.
- It reinforces self-confidence.

Praise can be offered publicly or privately. Naturally, if the praise is truly genuine, most people like the public recognition that goes with the honor of doing a good job. If you praise in public, do it uniformly so none of your employees feels left out of the picture.

USING CRITICISM

For most supervisors, criticism is far more difficult to handle than praise. You don't want to hurt anyone's feelings, and there is always concern about how the employee might react.

Examine a current problem you're having with an employee. Fill in the chart in preparation for applying the techniques that follow.

Employee name: _____
Title: _____
Description of the problem (only a description of the work-related problem—no mention of reasons for it or personality issues): ____

_____

_____

Possible causes (list all of the possible causes): _____

_____

_____

Key points to correct the problem: _____

_____

_____

_____

Keys to Effective Criticism

When you must criticize an employee's performance, follow these guidelines:

Limit Your Comments to the Behavior.   Don't label people as always stubborn, difficult, or easygoing. Don't criticize the person; focus on the task. Kelly, our nursing supervisor, would be far better off telling an employee that a specific report was late and letting the employee respond than berating the employee for tardiness in general.

Criticize as Quickly as Possible When You Discover a Problem.   The problem is fresh in the mind of the employee, so you'll generally get a more accurate response.

Listen Carefully to What the Employee Has to Say.   Get the employee's opinion; let the employee tell you what went wrong. Ask what he or she thinks the problem is. Don't prejudge an answer. Keep an open mind to what you hear.

Be Considerate.   Get your point across without being rude, brusque, or loud. Losing your temper may put the other person on the defensive and probably won't help you solve the problem or determine its cause.

Don't Present Criticism with Praise.   It sends a confusing message. There's often a tendency to want to say something nice to soften the blow. It doesn't work! It may blunt the criticism, but the praise means nothing—the employee only hears the bad news.

Don't Trap or Humiliate Employees.   For example, assume the hospital where Kelly works receives a complaint letter from a patient identifying a difficult nurse. Kelly should be straightforward in talking with the nurse about the problem. It would be a mistake to ask the nurse if he or she had a problem with a recent patient, and then trap the nurse by showing the letter.

Don't Blame Entire Departments for a Problem.   Mistakes happen. It may be someone's fault, but, as a supervisor, you should not generalize and say the entire group behaves poorly when in fact they don't.

Don't Play Psychiatrist and Try to Explain to an Employee Why an Unacceptable Act Occurred.   Unless you're a psychologist, leave it to the professionals. Your objective is to point out the problem, help find a solution, and prevent the problem from recurring.

Using the keys to effective criticism, make notes outlining the conversation you plan to have with your employee about the problem you described on page 68. _____

_____

_____

_____

_____

_____

In many cases, your best bet is to express criticism verbally, because written criticism may have unintended consequences:

- Written criticism is far more severe than verbal criticism.
- It becomes part of the employee's record, which could affect promotions and layoffs.
- The employee may not have an opportunity to respond or explain what occurred.
- The criticism remains an issue for a long time.
- Your comments may lack clear meaning because your tone of voice or any further explanation is not available to the reader.

Think carefully before you decide to prepare written criticism. The outcome may be more negative than productive.

What's the Best Time and Place to Criticize?

Depending on how severe the problem is, choose your office or workstation, the employee's office or workstation, or neutral ground. If you talk with an employee at his or her work location or a neutral site (such as a cafeteria, extra office, or lobby), you send a far less severe message than when you call the employee to your location. If the problem is, in fact, severe, the individual should come to you. It demonstrates just how serious the problem is. For a less formal and less intimidating mood, choose the employee's location or a neutral site.

Choose a time that's conducive to solving the problem as well. Don't deliver bad news (like criticism) just as the person is taking on some new task or project. It's also wise to avoid doing it over lunch or late in the day.

Generally the best time to criticize is early in the day so the employee can get on with his or her job and cool off by the end of the day.

Decide when and where you will talk with your employee about the problem you've identified on page 68. _____

_____
_____
_____

MANAGING CONFLICTS

Conflicts between your employees will occur. Many of them may seem unimportant, in the larger scheme of the organization, but they cannot be treated that way.

Practice the same techniques you would with criticism and praise. Listen carefully to each person involved. Judge the issues, not the personalities. Don't generalize or assume that the less competent or more "troublesome" person is the cause of the conflict.

After hearing the issues, make your decision (review Chapter 3 on decision making if needed) and handle any criticisms in the manner described in this chapter.

BALANCING PRAISE AND CRITICISM

As an effective supervisor, you should be using praise more than criticism. There should be more situations where praise is called for than criticism. If your employees respect you and your judgment, you should encounter fewer problems.

Have you been slow to praise in the past? If so, complete the following chart, take it to work with you, and put it into practice.

Employee Name	Recent Activity Worthy of Praise	Key Words I'll Use in Praising Him/Her

8

Chapter Checkpoints

✓ Do you regularly offer meaningful praise when it is deserved?

✓ When you criticize, do you listen carefully and criticize in private?

✓ Do you avoid mixing praise and criticism in all situations?

✓ Do you listen to all sides in a conflict, judging the issues and not the personalities involved?

9 | Delegating Work

This chapter will help you to:

- Learn the process of delegating work.
- Identify the types of tasks that should be delegated.
- Create a plan to make delegation work for you.

Rose was recently promoted to supervisor in a new branch office of a travel agency where she's worked for the past four years as an agent. As an agent, Rose was very competent and consistently led the office in sales. She developed a loyal client following that she is reluctant to give up.

She's finding the supervision aspects of her job to be very time consuming (filing reports, helping other agents and teaching them, meeting with suppliers). Rose is still trying to take care of some of her old clients and is, in fact, doing some of the work her employees should be doing because they're too slow or don't seem to do it properly. "It just seems easier to do it myself, but there isn't enough time in the day to manage it all," says Rose. ■

WHY MUST SUPERVISORS DELEGATE WORK?

One answer is obvious, as Rose found out: there isn't enough time in the day to do everything. There are other reasons as well:

- *Delegating work to others improves your time management and productivity.* Recall from Chapter 5 that one of the keys to successful time management is to eliminate tasks that others can do.

9

- *Delegating work is more efficient.* Supervising is a full-time job in most companies. Your role, as discussed in Chapter 1, is to supervise the activities of others. You and your subordinates doing the proper job is more efficient for the company as a whole.

- *Delegating work develops the skills and abilities of others.* Doing the work yourself often seems faster and easier because your subordinates have not yet learned the task as well as you have. They never will, if you don't give them a chance. Valuable efficient employees will make you look good as well.

- *Delegation increases job satisfaction for your employees.* It shows you're interested in developing their skills and trusting them with responsibility.

- *It helps you better evaluate your employees.* If you're always stepping in, you can't be a fair judge of others' work. After all, they've not had a chance to prove themselves. As a supervisor, you're far better off supporting your employees' efforts and helping them, rather than taking over the task yourself.

Why Avoid Delegation?

With so many good reasons for delegating work, why are some supervisors reluctant to do it?

Check off the reasons that make you hesitate to delegate work:

☐ *Less power and influence.* If you derived a sense of power and influence from your work prior to being a supervisor, it's quite easy to feel a sense of loss when someone else is doing the task. For many, giving up a task feels like taking away some of their own self-worth.

☐ *Less control over the job.* Someone else is now in control of the task. As a supervisor, you can find it frustrating to know that your employees are doing what you used to do and maybe learning to do it better.

☐ *Giving up the "fun" stuff.* Every job has favorite elements for every employee. Perhaps Rose truly enjoyed meeting and talking with new clients and now rarely gets to do that as a supervisor. She feels frustrated when she sees other people doing what she enjoyed so much. Perhaps when she sees others doing things differently, she sometimes thinks they're doing things not as well as she used to.

☐ *Other reasons.* _____

THE PROCESS OF DELEGATION

Delegation begins with understanding the goal of your job and the jobs of the people who work for you. If there is no written description for their positions, take the time to write one. Doing so can help both you and your employees focus on what you're all trying to accomplish.

Once that is done, create a list of the tasks for which people are currently responsible. In the travel agency, the list might include meeting with

9

clients, answering questions, offering ideas, selling ideas, and collecting funds.

Set goals for each of your employees for the tasks they must handle. Let your employees know what you expect of them. At the same time, be sensitive to their needs. Make sure they understand what you're asking of them and what they'll have to do. If they're not sure what task needs to be done or how to do it, it will be difficult for them to meet the goal. When you delegate a task for the first time, it's especially critical to communicate clearly.

It's also critical to supervise your employee's performance and make sure they learn to do the task correctly. We'll cover training in more detail in Chapter 10.

WHAT TYPES OF TASKS CAN BE DELEGATED?

You can't delegate your entire job away, so what should you delegate?

Start by Listing All of Your Own Tasks

If necessary, keep a time log for several weeks to see what you do on a daily basis. You may want to use the log you started in Chapter 5. Start your list here:

_____

_____

_____

_____

Start with the Most Routine Tasks

These are the day-to-day things that could easily be learned and handled by someone else. Note your most routine tasks here:

_____

_____

_____

_____

Get Rid of the Trivial Tasks

These tasks are not worth your time as a supervisor. Again, be objective. Don't hang onto trivial tasks that are fun or easy. Your time as a supervisor is too valuable to waste on these. Note the trivial tasks here:

_____

_____

_____

_____

Give Up the Time-Consuming Tasks that Others Could Handle

Even if the task is one you truly enjoy, you cannot afford to spend a lot of time on it as a supervisor. Note time-consuming tasks that others could handle here:

_____

_____

_____

_____

Look for Parts of Your Job that Could Be Easily Taught to Others

What do you do that could be handled by others with just a little instruction? Note easy-to-teach tasks here:

_____

_____

_____

_____

CREATING A DELEGATION PLAN

Once you've decided to delegate work, here are three key rules to follow.

1. **Don't take an assignment back after you've delegated it.** Help the person learn how to do it and be patient, but don't take over for him or her. Doing so demoralizes the conscientious worker who

is really trying and gives the lazy worker a perfect out: "Do a bad job and let the supervisor do it for you."

2. Encourage your employees to learn and make their own decisions about how to do the task. Be patient but, at the same time, insist that the task be done correctly.

3. Make sure you've clearly defined what you want your employees to do and they understand what you expect. Ideally, you'll be able to involve them in setting the objectives for the task.

Now it's your turn. Below is the formula for creating your own delegation plan. Originally presented in 1983[1], it has stood the test of time and is an excellent tool for creating your own plan.

A Plan for Delegating Work

1. Make a list of the tasks you're responsible for doing.

2. Create a time log for each task.

3. By employee, list the skills and talents your various employees have. What do they do well?

4. Place the name of a staff member by each of your tasks from item 1.

5. Write instructions for the task.

6. Have a backup plan in case employees are truly unable to do the task.

7. Periodically, review the tasks that have been delegated to see how people are doing.

Sample Chart

For example, Rose at the travel agency would start by making a list of her own tasks to delegate, and the skills and talents of each employee. She would then set up the chart as shown.

---

[1] *Back to Basics Management* (New York: Culligan, Deakins & Young, Published Facts on File, Inc., 1983).

	Employees			
	Sue	Don	Mary	Kim
Rose's Tasks				
Answer phone	1			
Greet walk-in prospects		1		2
Check messages	1			
Organize files			2	1

1 is her first delegation choice; 2 is her second choice.

Now it's your turn. List the tasks you're responsible for performing. Refer to your time log and previous exercises if necessary.

My Tasks

_____

_____

_____

_____

_____

List the names of your employees and write a brief description of their talents. For example, an employee with excellent handwriting may be a good person to prepare all the signs you need but don't have time to do yourself.

9

Name	**Special Skills**
_____	_____
_____	_____
_____	_____
_____	_____
_____	_____

On the next page, list the tasks you do that can be delegated down the left side of the chart. List the employees' names across the top of the chart. Put a star or 1 in each space where the person is the best suited to do the job. Put a 2 next to your backup person, if you can identify one.

Employees _____ _____ _____ _____ _____

My tasks:

1. _____ _____ _____ _____ _____ _____
2. _____ _____ _____ _____ _____ _____
3. _____ _____ _____ _____ _____ _____
4. _____ _____ _____ _____ _____ _____
5. _____ _____ _____ _____ _____ _____
6. _____ _____ _____ _____ _____ _____
7. _____ _____ _____ _____ _____ _____
8. _____ _____ _____ _____ _____ _____
9. _____ _____ _____ _____ _____ _____
10. _____ _____ _____ _____ _____ _____

Chapter Checkpoints

✓ Have you decided which of your daily tasks can realistically be delegated to other people (including the ones you enjoy doing but could be done by others)?

✓ Do you set realistic goals for your employees when you assign tasks?

✓ Do you carefully explain what you want an employee to do each time you delegate a task?

✓ Have you completed your own delegation chart and started delegating work based on your chart?

10 | Training and Team Building

This chapter will help you to:

- Review a variety of training methods.
- Consider ways of making training work.
- Analyze training efforts.
- Overcome common obstacles to team building.

Bill is supervisor in an automotive parts distribution center. He supervises a staff that includes inventory clerks, shipping clerks, and people from several support functions. His company has experienced relatively high turnover in recent years, and Bill must devote a good percentage of his time to training new employees or recently transferred employees.

He finds himself explaining how to do things over and over to the same people. The information just doesn't seem to stick. He also has a difficult time getting employees involved enough in their jobs and the company to do a good job. He would love to find a way to train people more effectively. ■

TRAINING METHODS: COMMUNICATING WITH EMPLOYEES

Think back to your school days. Do you remember some teachers who seemed much better than others at teaching? Personality may have been part of why you learned; that is, you liked that teacher. Yet, when you talked to friends, they didn't always share your view. They learned more from teachers you thought weren't as good.

One common reason for this difference is in teaching methods. Some

of us respond more to auditory methods (to hearing information). Some of us respond better to visual methods (to seeing information). Most of us respond best to some combination.

Variations of auditory and visual methods can be used in job training. When you have to train new people, you need to be sensitive to differences in learning style. Try to use as many methods as possible with your employees.

Review the following methods and take a few minutes to think about your own teaching style. Could you implement these methods to become a more effective trainer at work?

Put a check next to methods that you've used, and a star next to methods that you'd like to try with your employees in the future.

☐ *Doing the job.* If it's a simple task, one method is on-the-job training. The employee tries the task, and you correct the mistakes. This method should be limited to simple tasks so the employee doesn't get frustrated.

☐ *Demonstration.* Perform the task and explain it so the employee can observe the correct method. This is how most medical schools train doctors. They certainly wouldn't want to start with on-the-job training.

☐ *Conversational questioning.* As in an informal quiz, you present the task by asking questions. For example, Bill might ask a new shipping clerk why he uses certain types of packing material with different products. The answer may be "for different levels of protection." By posing a question, Bill gets the employee to think about the reasons for doing something. Understanding rationale makes procedures logical and sensible to the new employee and easier to learn.

☐ *Role playing.* If the task involves communicating with others, as in customer service, consider role playing. One perosn plays the customer calling with a problem, and the new employee tries to solve the problem in a realistic situation. As a supervisor, you can step in with questions and comments to help the person solve the problem.

☐ *Open discussion.* Usually combined with demonstration of how to do a task, open discussion gives the employee an opportunity to ask questions and to understand why something is done a certain way. It also provides an opportunity for the supervisor to relate the new task to previous tasks, making a connection to something more familiar.

10

REACHING THE EMPLOYEE

Here are some tips for putting training methods into practice.

Plan Ahead

Before you start teaching others, organize yourself first.

Use Visual and Auditory Approaches

Visual approaches include demonstrations, videotape or film, slides and overheads, and books and pamphlets. Auditory methods include audiotapes to take home or open discussions among you and fellow employees. Computers provide both auditory and visual information and can be an excellent teaching tool.

Use Methods that Allow the Learner to Respond (Interactive Teaching)

Some examples include audiotapes that tell people to stop and complete an action or computer programs that require completing steps before continuing.

MAKING TRAINING WORK

What's in it for me? That's the question your employees will legitimately ask. Why should they learn to do something that offers nothing for them? As a supervisor, you need to reach out to your employees and find the answer to that question. If you don't provide a good answer, the training may lose its effectiveness over the long run.

Recognize Their Own Experiences.   Can you relate the training to employee interests and past experiences?

Promote Professionalism.   Being good at their jobs should be a source of pride for employees. Promote the attitude that everyone benefits when a company does better as a result of team efforts.

Professionalism Leads to Self-Development.   Most people take pride in what they do when they feel confident about themselves. They're more willing to take on new challenges, and they find self-development is truly in their interest.

A great deal of research has shown that self-development, recognition, and a sense of achievement on the job tend to outrank money as a motivator, at least in most developed nations. Confidence and skills improvement go a long way in helping people in these areas.

Let the Employee Know How He or She Is Doing. This is especially needed if the task is new to the employee. Feedback lets employees know if they're on the right tract, corrects any errors, and builds confidence.

Make the Objectives of the Task Clear; Emphasize Improvements. Tell the person how well he or she is doing individually, as opposed to how well the person is doing compared to your best people.

REVIEW THE TRAINING PROCESS

Don't assume that once you've explained something it's understood. Be ready to evaluate your own training. Use this checklist to determine how well your training worked.

Periodically ask yourself these questions:

1. Was the job completed correctly and in a timely manner?
2. How well was the job done?
3. What problems needed to be addressed? Are they likely to occur with other employees as well?
4. What new techniques or ideas emerged? (Perhaps the employee had another way of doing the task that worked equally well or better.)
5. How did the employee react? Is he or she ready for new tasks and advancement on the job?

DEVELOPING YOUR OWN MODEL

How can you apply what you've learned about training to your own supervisory job? List a task that you must teach people to do. Then compare it against this checklist to see which methods will work. Are you using the most appropriate methods in an effective combination?

Task: _____

Method	Will Work	Have Tried
Formal presentation	_____	_____
On-the-job	_____	_____

(continued)

Task: _____

Method	Will Work	Have Tried
Demonstration	_____	_____
Conversational questioning	_____	_____
Role playing	_____	_____
Open discussion	_____	_____
Flipchart	_____	_____
Slides/overheads	_____	_____
Film/video	_____	_____
Audiotapes	_____	_____
Computer training	_____	_____
Books/pamphlets	_____	_____
Other(s)	_____	_____

TEAM BUILDING: DEALING WITH THE OBSTACLES

As we saw in Chapter 1, a supervisor's major role is to keep people moving in a common direction.

At the same time, we've seen the importance of understanding your employees as individuals and appreciating their differences. Their needs must be met if you expect them to behave like a team.

For supervisors, team building means meeting two goals: getting your employees to think and act as a team for the benefit of the company, and satisfying their individual job needs.

Here are some common impediments to team building, along with some ideas about how to overcome them. Check the ones that apply to your situation.

☐ *Frequent disagreements.* Some people like to argue, while others feel they truly have something worth arguing about. You need to listen carefully for valuable information and reduce the argumentative behavior, as it can be disruptive.

☐ *Shy people may be afraid to suggest ideas.* As a result, they tend to resent things that don't go their way. You may need to draw them out and make sure they understand their role and purpose as part of a team. Otherwise, they may be too embarrassed to tell you what they need.

☐   *Some people fear all new methods or ideas.* They automatically say no to anything new. If that's the case, try to find out why they're objecting. If a new method is superior to an old one, draw them out on the subject. Force them to think about why they're resisting the change.

☐   *Some employees seem bored or disinterested.* Get people involved in training to prevent the boredom and disinterest that may result from only listening or watching others. Bored employees may not learn well.

☐   *"Know-it-alls" tend to dominate.* Handle the know-it-alls carefully. They may, in fact, have a lot of knowledge and merely want recognition. In other cases, they may be seeking attention. Give them some attention, but don't be afraid to correct them diplomatically if they're wrong.

10

Chapter Checkpoints

✓ Do you try to use a varitey of training methods to teach new skills?

✓ Do you use both visual and auditory approaches to training?

✓ Do you make your training interactive?

✓ Do you explain why a task is done a particular way?

✓ Do you provide feedback to employees?

✓ Do you evaluate how well your own training efforts work?

✓ Do you foster a team approach rather than a competitive one among your employees?

11 | The Consummate Supervisor

This chapter will help you to:

- Take a closer look at your employees' needs.
- Understand what your company expects of you as a supervisor.
- Evaluate and improve your supervisory skills in the future.

What do your employees really want? What motivates them to follow your leadership and your direction? What does the company want? What can or should you be doing to improve your own skills to be a better supervisor?

Knowing the answers to these questions will help you become the consummate supervisor. ■

UNDERSTANDING THE NEEDS OF YOUR EMPLOYEES

What do your employees want out of a job? We considered this question in Chapter 2, but now let's take a broader view.

Surveys have often shown a disparity between what people want out of a job and what their bosses think they want. Many supervisors and managers rank money and job security at the top of the list of what they feel their employees want from a job. And yet, most employee surveys put money and job security somewhere between third place and sixth place—behind such issues as appreciation for good work, recognition, feeling involved with the company, and a comfortable work environment.

Does this disparity surprise you? We often forget what drove us when we were in our employees' positions. For that matter, we may even forget what drives us in our current position. It's usually the same: supervisors seek more responsibility and recognition for a job well done, not just a raise.

EXPLAINING PEOPLE'S NEEDS

Two psychologists have studied people's needs to explain the reasons behind them. Abraham Maslow developed what is known as the *theory of self-actualization*. Very simply stated, the theory of self-actualization describes the needs of people in terms of a *hierarchy*. Maslow's hierarchy moves from the most basic needs to higher needs: safety/security needs, physiological needs, social needs, esteem needs, self-actualization needs. In other words, we must first meet our most basic needs—those at the bottom of the hierarchy—before our needs shift to a higher level.

For example, a person who is starving and has no place to sleep is probably not as concerned with what people think about him or her as with eating and finding shelter. Those are basic needs. Once that person has established a safe place to sleep and a steady diet, his or her needs move up the hierarchy. The person then becomes concerned with what people think of him or her.

In our society, the majority of people are near the top of the hierarchy. Maslow describes the top levels as self-realization and self-actualization. In other words, we respond to recognition, a sense of responsibility and achievement, and so on, since our basic needs have been met.

Does this view make sense to you? Does it help explain the results of so many employer and employee surveys? Does it explain your own behavior on the job? Write your comments here: _____

_____

_____

_____

_____

Here's another view. Frederick Herzberg presents us with the *two-factor theory*. Simply stated, job elements are classified as one of two factors: they are either *motivators* (things that motivate us) or *hygienes* (conditions that are basic and must be present).

For example, good lighting in your place of work is a hygiene. It must be present, but it doesn't motivate anyone to come to work. A promotion or recognition is a motivator. We work for those kinds of honors.

Interestingly enough, salaries are considered a hygiene. Would you go to work if your paycheck was not assured? It doesn't motivate us; it has to be there. A new raise may be a motivator briefly, but the salary increase quickly becomes expected and, therefore, a hygiene.

Does this make sense to you? Does it help explain your employees' needs? Your own needs?

Write your own needs here: _____

_____

_____

Write your employees' needs here: _____

_____

_____

11

TAKE ANOTHER LOOK

As we saw in Chapter 2, your employees have a variety of needs and goals that you need to consider. Some of the most common higher-level needs are listed below. Try to determine which needs are most important for your employees. Which are most important to you?

- *Security*—a sense of job security and stability; not too many changes; a stable work environment; likes routine tasks.

Employees' names: _____
_____
_____

- *Social*—needs to be with other people, to talk with them and exchange ideas; dislikes work that is solitary with no other contact for long periods of time.

Employees' names: _____
_____
_____

- *Status*—wants to be recognized as someone important; likes to be considered influential and a source of good ideas.

Employees' names: _____
_____
_____

- *Independence*—wants to be left alone and trusted to work alone; feels very confident and secure and doesn't want to be bothered with teamwork issues.

Employees' names: _____
_____
_____

- *Mature/self-actualizing*—the ideal employee, who blends a mix of curiosity and interest in what's going on and at the same time is willing to take charge of a task with a good deal of self-confidence.

Employees' names: _____
_____
_____

Here are five tips for dealing with all of these employee types.

1. **Be courteous and friendly.** Express your interest in what they do and let them know you care about them as people as well as workers.

2. **Offer assistance when needed.** Help them develop their own skills but be available to offer help.

3. **Listen patiently to their ideas and what they have to say.** You can learn from them and, at the same time, demonstrate a real interest in their needs.

4. **Express your interest in them** by observing their work and providing feedback on how they do.

5. **Make your goals reasonable** and let them know what you expect of them. Again, be careful to allow for individual differences in what motivates people and what's important to them.

How do you think you are doing at putting these tips into practice? Note any of the five tips that you'd like to apply more conscientiously:

_____

_____

_____

_____

UNDERSTANDING THE NEEDS OF
YOUR COMPANY

Your company expects you to supervise people and the work they do. As a supervisor, you take direction from others and implements tasks through the people who work for you.

Your company's expectations of you may include:

▪ Staying aware of the big picture. Don't focus only on your own department or immediate responsibilities. Be sensitive to what's going on in other departments and to meeting the needs of the company as a whole.

▪ Creating a productive environment for your employees. Practicing good supervision skills that will lead to productive employees is a basic requirement for the job.

- Making decisions on your own and exercising leadership and good judgment.

- Implementing new programs and methods while gaining employee acceptance.

- Communicating effectively with your employees to keep them informed about company policies and procedures.

- Teaching your employees to be effective at what they do and helping them develop their own skills.

It's a tall order for any supervisor, but this list should be a part of your own job goals as well.

Look back at the business goals you set for yourself in Chapter 1. Do they reflect all of the expectations of a supervisor that we've just discussed? Note here any expectations that need to be incorporated into your goals:

_____

_____

_____

_____

_____

_____

Supervision is a challenging and rewarding job that combines many skills and talents. Like everything else, supervision skills and techniques will change and evolve. Stay on top of your profession by constantly improving your own skills. The consummate supervisor is always on the lookout for better ways to improve job performance, including supervising.

11

Chapter Checkpoints

✓ Do you know what motivates you as a supervisor?

✓ Do you help your employees develop their own skills while offering assistance when it's needed?

✓ Do you set reasonable goals for each of your employees and communicate what you expect of them?

✓ Are you working to meet the needs of the company as a whole, instead of just pursuing the interests of your own department?

✓ Are you creating a productive working environment for your employees?

✓ Do you have to update and improve your supervisory skills?

Post-Test

So *now* how do you feel about being a supervisor? How do you feel about your ability to perform the job well? Take this self-assessment test and decide for yourself. Plan to work on the areas where you rate yourself as needing improvement.

Consider making copies of the test and sharing it with some of your employees to see how they would rate you. After all, communication is part of effective supervision.

	Always	Sometimes	Never
1. I write a list of personal and business goals and keep it updated.	_____	_____	_____
2. I keep my goals prioritized in order of importance so I know where I am headed.	_____	_____	_____
3. I know, from my employees' point of view, what is important to them in their work.	_____	_____	_____
4. I feel confident in directing the actions of the people that work for me.	_____	_____	_____
5. I am comfortable making decisions on my own.	_____	_____	_____
6. I feel comfortable communicating with my employees.	_____	_____	_____
7. I feel comfortable communicating with my superiors.	_____	_____	_____
8. I focus on developing the skills of my employees.	_____	_____	_____

	Always	Sometimes	Never
9. I keep an open mind when making decisions that will affect my employees.	_____	_____	_____
10. I am careful not to take sides in disputes.	_____	_____	_____
11. When I make a decision, I think about its implications.	_____	_____	_____
12. I try to gain employee acceptance of my decisions without forcing them.	_____	_____	_____
13. When we implement a new procedure, I carefully observe how well it is working.	_____	_____	_____
14. I explain the reasons for new procedures rather than just explaining that a new procedure exists.	_____	_____	_____
15. I am patient with employees when they are learning a new procedure.	_____	_____	_____
16. I build in contingency plans for new procedures in case they don't work.	_____	_____	_____
17. I always know how I'm spending my time and make sure I use it effectively.	_____	_____	_____
18. I prioritize my work on a daily basis.	_____	_____	_____
19. I listen carefully to my employees.	_____	_____	_____

	Always	Sometimes	Never
20. I am sensitive to cultural differences.	_____	_____	_____
21. I communicate clearly and am well understood by my employees			
In writing	_____	_____	_____
Verbally	_____	_____	_____
22. When I hold a meeting, I plan the agenda in advance and let everyone know what it is.	_____	_____	_____
23. I prepare in advance for individual meetings or meetings with a group.	_____	_____	_____
24. I praise my employees when they do a good job.	_____	_____	_____
25. I avoid mixing praise and criticism.	_____	_____	_____
26. I keep personal issues out of criticism and focus only on behavior	_____	_____	_____
27. I criticize in private only.	_____	_____	_____
28. I listen carefully when criticizing to hear the employee's point of view.	_____	_____	_____
29. I make a conscious effort to delegate work to others so they may learn.	_____	_____	_____
30. I am careful to delegate work that is best suited to employees.	_____	_____	_____

	Always	Sometimes	Never
31. I set goals for employees when they take on new tasks.	_____	_____	_____
32. I use a variety of training methods to teach my employees new tasks.	_____	_____	_____
33. I appeal to the self-interest of my employees in wanting to do a better job.	_____	_____	_____
34. I am sensitive to my employees as individuals and try to help them meet their own work goals.	_____	_____	_____
35. I am sensitive to the needs of the company and retain a big-picture perspective on company goals.	_____	_____	_____

How did you do? Where do you need to improve? To find your score, give yourself a three for each Always, a two for each Sometimes, and a one for each Never.

90 or higher	**Congratulations!** You're on your way to success as a supervisor.
76–89	**You're above average** and have developed some of the critical management and supervisory skills needed to become an excellent supervisor.
66–75	**You're doing an acceptable job but could improve in some key areas.**
65 or less	**You still have work ahead of you to become comfortable at supervising.**

Keep this book handy as a reference and use it when you need assistance. Use the Skill Maintenance checklist on the inside back cover to assess yourself periodically.

THE BUSINESS SKILLS EXPRESS SERIES

This growing series of books addresses a broad range of key business skills and topics to meet the needs of employees, human resource departments, and training consultants.

To obtain information about these and other Business Skills Express books, please call Business One IRWIN toll free at: 1-800-634-3966.

Skill Maintenance

Use this checklist to measure your success periodically after completing *The New Supervisor*. The skills you learned need to be practiced, and with practice, they will become an integral part of your professional life. Enter today's date below, and using a calendar select dates 3, 6, and 12 months ahead. Note the dates in the columns below and in your daily planner to remind yourself to return to the checklist. Refer to the chapter reference for any item you checked no.

Today's date: _____	Date ____ 3 months		Date ____ 6 months		Date ____ 1 year		Chapter Reference
	Yes	No	Yes	No	Yes	No	
1. I have written down my business and personal goals for at least one year.							1
2. I use a worksheet comparing my objectives with employee objectives and have set up a course of action to reach our combined objectives.							2
3. I have my own copy of the decision planner and use it for key decisions.							3
4. I have created a chart for following changes in my employees' behavior.							4
5. I have a time log to periodically evaluate my use of time.							5
6. I monitor how my employees react to information and how well I communicate verbally and in writing.							6
7. I have reduced the number of meetings I must attend.							7
8. I always praise in public and criticize in private and keep my praise meaningful.							8
9. I have not taken on any new projects that could be delegated to my employees.							9
10. I have instilled a sense of team effort in my employees and made sure they are able to do their jobs.							10
11. I maintain a balance between the needs of my employees, my company, and myself.							11